Steam in the West Riding

# Steam in the West Riding

J. S. Whiteley

and

G. W. Morrison

with an introduction by David Joy

**DAVID & CHARLES**

NEWTON ABBOT · LONDON · NORTH POMFRET (VT) · VANCOUVER

ISBN 0 7153 7121 5
Library of Congress Catalog Card Number 75-26365

Set and printed in Great Britain
by Biddles Ltd, Guildford, Surrey
for David & Charles (Publishers) Limited
Brunel House Newton Abbot Devon


Published in the United States of America
by David & Charles Inc
North Pomfret Vermont 05053 USA


Published in Canada
by Douglas David & Charles Limited
1875 Welch Street North Vancouver BC

## Introduction *by David Joy*

It is a wet, West Riding night. Flickering gaslights reflect eerily in murky pools formed among the cracked platform flags. A few figures huddle against the dirty, down-at-heel station buildings, seeking protection from the rain and a chilly wind sweeping unchallenged across the gaunt Pennine heights. With heavy raincoats fully buttoned, they stare disconsolately across the town as musings on railway unpunctuality become clouded by meditations on urban landscape. Waiting impatiently for a train is not a time to see beauty in tiers of dark, Dickensian mills or rows of sooty black terrace houses climbing out of the narrow valley towards the wide sky. Thoughts return to earth as the station drifts rather than erupts into activity. Bells sound in the signal box, red lights change to green, a porter ambles on to the platform. Away in the distance can just be heard the unmistakable beat of a locomotive working hard as it pounds up the 1 in 120 gradient. Soon a 'Black Five' emerges from the night, shuts off steam and halts to the accompaniment of squealing brakes and hissing cylinder cocks. Doors open and quickly close as passengers scurry into the train like half-drowned rabbits making a bolt for their warren. A whistle blows and wheels momentarily slip on wet rails before the engine takes a grip of its load and chugs purposefully towards the tunnel mouth yawning only yards from the platform end. The blur of lights vanishes, the porter shuffles off the platform and the station resumes its slumbers.

The scene is Halifax in the late 1950s, in many ways epitomising the West Riding steam railway in its teatime of life and yet in other ways unique. For an outstanding characteristic of this most individual portion of a remarkable county has always been its refusal to conform or to be moulded into a cohesive pattern. No two settlements are alike, and no town has achieved total dominance over its neighbours. This position is likely to apply for many years to come, even though the West Riding ceased to exist as an administrative unit in 1974 and was savagely split between several new authorities—mainly North Yorkshire and the metropolitan counties of South and West Yorkshire. It is, however, still very much in being as an historical entity and for this reason is referred to in the present tense in these pages. Its stubbornness, individuality and determination not to create a focal point have greatly influenced the development of the region's railways. In the pre-Grouping era conurbations outside London were generally dominated by two or three companies, but in the West Riding the spoils were divided between no fewer than seven major railways and a host of joint lines, all competing for prominence and all with their own highly distinctive flavour. Furthermore, at Grouping the area's railways were roughly shared between the LMS and LNER, and the majority of joint lines remained such, so that this absence of uniformity persisted until nationalisation and well beyond.

Two of the three Anglo-Scottish main lines cut through the West Riding. The East Coast route, which as far as this area is concerned achieved its final form in 1871, curves through the marshy plains of south-east Yorkshire before almost losing itself in the maze of marshalling yards heralding the approach to Doncaster. More than anywhere else in the West Riding this was a railway town, the main source of employment for many a decade being 'the Plant', principal locomotive works of the Great Northern Railway and later the LNER. At the north end of Doncaster station the lines to Leeds and Hull diverge, and the main line heads like an arrow into the Vale of York and past Shaftholme Junction, once the frontier between the Great Northern and North Eastern railways but now merely of historical importance. Only Selby with its sweeping curves and swing-bridge over the Ouse punctuates an otherwise featureless passage across arable land to York itself.

The Midland route to Scotland is altogether a different affair. It enters the West Riding underground in the depths of Bradway tunnel, penetrating the watershed between the Drone and Sheaf valleys. At Dore & Totley the line to Chinley and Manchester goes off to the west and plunges into Totley tunnel, at 3 miles 950 yd the longest in Britain after the Severn. A descent from the outlying hills of the Peak District takes the main line into the

*Frontispiece* The Waverley, the Midland route express from St Pancras to Edinburgh via Leeds and Carlisle, now but a memory, heads northwards round Shipley triangle behind Holbeck rebuilt Scot No 46109 *Royal Engineer* on 10 May 1961. *G. W. Morrison*

environs of Sheffield, the West Riding's largest city, where the Midland station at Pond Street straddles the confluence of the Porter and Sheaf rivers and is very much in the bottom of a hole.

At Rotherham the original main line from Chesterfield via Killamarsh and Treeton is joined, but the railway continues to be lined by a near-continuous chain of steelworks and factories for several more miles until it leaves the Don Valley at Swinton. Here the former Swinton & Knottingley Joint branches off to the north, handling many cross-country expresses making the long journey from Bristol and beyond to York and Newcastle. On the main line there is little chance to see green fields before the Barnsley coalfield is entered and a succession of spoil heaps mars the approaches to Darfield, Cudworth—with its one-time maze of junctions—and Royston. Reputedly the deepest cutting in Britain at Chevet precedes the entry into Normanton, once nicknamed 'the Crewe of the coalfields' and in the 1840s among the most important railway junctions in the country. Subsequently by-passed by new construction it had a second lease of life in the pre-dining car era as a refreshment stop for Anglo-Scottish expresses. Today the quarter of a mile long island platform and massive buildings where passengers once invited instant indigestion by gobbling five courses in 20 min are pathetic remnants of a different age.

There are more collieries on each side of the line as it begins to run into Leeds, a city which caused feuds almost without number among the early railway companies. On summer Saturdays certain Midland main line trains avoid calling here altogether by taking the curve at Holbeck, but otherwise all through services from the south to Scotland reverse at Leeds City.

For almost the first time since leaving the Peak District, industrial surroundings give way to relatively open country as the railway heads up the Aire Valley, cutting through a spur of high ground by a ¾-mile long tunnel at Thackley. At Shipley, lines diverge to the south to terminate at Bradford (Forster Square), the Midland's dream of forming a shorter main line by means of a Royston—Dewsbury—Bradford link never having reached fruition. The hills begin to close in beyond the mill towns of Bingley and Keighley, while Skipton sees the last vestiges of industrialisation and marks the entry into a totally different world.

Hedges give way to drystone walls and limestone country as the line deserts the valley of the Aire for that of the Ribble. At Hellifield the important link with Blackburn and central Lancashire trails in from the south, and at Settle Junction the Carnforth and Morecambe line branches off to the west. But it is the route ahead that rivets the attention of all enthusiasts, as this is the start of what many consider to be the finest railway in England. The 72 miles from Settle to Carlisle have become a legend in their own lifetime, for surely nowhere else does a main line cut through so difficult a countryside in such a magnificent way. The first dozen miles, known as 'the long drag', climb almost continuously at 1 in 100 to the head of Ribblesdale where the Three Peaks of Ingleborough, Penyghent and Whernside are all visible. Thereafter viaduct follows tunnel in quick succession as the line strides across windy Chapel-le-Dale, plunges through Blea Moor, clings to a ledge high above the green floor of Dentdale and then enters Garsdale where the highest water troughs in the world were formerly situated. Here the railway leaves the West Riding at one of the major watersheds of northern England where rivers rising within yards of one another enter the sea at estuaries as far apart as the Solway, Lune and Humber.

Almost throughout the steam age motive power on the Midland main line varied north and south of Leeds. For most of the post-war period Holbeck Royal Scots tended to monopolise the expresses north of Leeds, which basically comprised a London—Glasgow and a London-Edinburgh sleeper, the morning Leeds-Glasgow service, the Waverley and the Thames-Clyde express from London. Jubilees, Clans and Britannias also played their part, however, and just before dieselisation a startling innovation occurred when A3 Pacifics displaced from the East Coast route began to work off Holbeck shed.

South of Leeds the gradients were less demanding, and so the more frequent services were mainly in the hands of class 5 4-6-0s and Jubilees. Again, there was a change in the closing years of steam when Royal Scots, no longer required on the West Coast route, were moved to Kentish town shed, meaning that for a while this class dominated passenger haulage on the whole of the Midland main line. Of special interest were the trains from St Pancras and the West Country, including the Devonian, which terminated at Bradford. Often loading to 14 coaches, they were purposefully handled by deceptively powerful 4MT 2-6-4Ts for the short haul between Leeds and Bradford. Much of the substantial freight traffic on the Midland route remained in the charge of 4F 0-6-0s until a surprisingly late date, with Stanier Class 5s and 8F 2-8-0s grappling with the heavier trains.

There was one other route from London into the West Riding which tends to be over-looked by steam devotees, partly because it was in decline even before nationalisation but also because the most interesting portion was electrified in 1954. This was the ex-Great Central main line from London (Marylebone) to Sheffield (Victoria), where steam gave way to electric haulage for the climb over the Pennines and through Woodhead tunnel to Manchester. One of the most interesting trains of the day was the South Yorkshireman from Marylebone to Bradford (Exchange) via Huddersfield. It diverged from the Manchester line at Penistone, following a route which cuts across the grain of some very attractive countryside by a string of tunnels, bridges and viaducts culminating in the magnificent structure at Lockwood, 34 arches towering 136ft above the river Holme. There was also the unofficially named Continental from Harwich (Parkeston Quay) which regularly brought into Sheffield a B17 4-6-0, a class otherwise very much confined to East Anglia.

The two other trans-Pennine routes had much more to offer the steam enthusiast. The former London & North Western main line into Yorkshire climbs out of Manchester via Stalybridge to Standedge, where the one double-line and two single-line bores were famous for their unique water troughs actually inside the tunnels. A gradual descent leads to Huddersfield, notable as being the only station in the whole of the West Riding with any real architectural merit, after which there was formerly a choice of approaches to Leeds. The present-day route briefly shares tracks with the Calder Valley main line through Mirfield and then diverges by way of Dewsbury and Morley tunnel before curving into Leeds City. In more halcyon days this approach could be very congested and so certain expresses were switched to the Leeds New Line, pursuing a serpentine and steeply-graded path through the Spen Valley and the 1¼-mile Gildersome tunnel but one completely free of junctions until it joined the original route by an impressive fly-over at Farnley. The Liverpool-Newcastle expresses which form the mainstay of traffic over the Standedge line have always been heavily loaded and in steam days were often double-headed by a pair of Royal Scots from Edge Hill or a Scot and a Patriot. Other Liverpool-Newcastle services gave the passenger a more eventful journey by reversing at Leeds and taking the former Leeds Northern line with its passage of Bramhope tunnel, graceful sweep across Wharfedale beyond Arthington, excruciatingly curved approach to Crimple viaduct and gentle ascent through the outskirts of Harrogate. The line beyond here has now gone but once crossed the Nidd and Ure to serve Ripon, the smallest of our cities, before reaching Northallerton.

The ex Lancashire & Yorkshire route into the West Riding is somehow far less auspicious—it is constrained by the almost gorge-like nature of the upper Calder Valley, sports numerous junctions and speed restrictions and on the motive power front has never risen above class 5s, Jubilees and the occasional Patriot. It pierces the watershed by the shortest of the trans-Pennine tunnels at Summit and then descends to Todmorden, where the line climbing over Copy Pit to Burnley had great photographic potential in the steam era and still provides an interesting link from the West Riding to Preston and Blackpool. A succession of short tunnels punctuates the passage of the narrowest part of the Calder Valley, which begins to widen out at Sowerby Bridge. Here trains from Liverpool and Manchester to York followed a portion of the main line now sadly closed to regular passenger traffic, passing Mirfield, Wakefield (Kirkgate) and Normanton before traversing ex North Eastern metals through Castleford and Church Fenton.

The Bradford portions, detached from Leeds trains at Low Moor or Halifax, dropped precipitously into the city's Exchange station, while what was normally the main part of the train continued over former Great Northern tracks into the cramped confines of Leeds Central. This latter section of line served a dual role for it also forms a vital link in the approach to Bradford from King's Cross. Expresses leave the East Coast route at Doncaster, taking the one-time West Riding & Grimsby joint line through the coalfield and entering Wakefield (Westgate) over the famous '99-arch' viaduct across the Calder. Here many steam-hauled trains detached a Bradford portion, which was worked along the line climbing to over 700 ft above sea level as it passed through Morley Top and other windswept stations on the ridge separating the Aire and Calder valleys. The rest of the train continued into Leeds Central, where in fact some services would reverse and go on to Bradford through Stanningley instead of dividing at Wakefield. Named trains from King's Cross terminating at Bradford were the West Riding, White Rose and Yorkshire Pullman.

The main lines of the West Riding are complex enough, but there are also numerous secondary routes well above branch line status which clearly can only be referred to in passing in a brief introduction of this kind. There are the many lines which formerly ran into Barnsley, including the two parallel approaches from Sheffield through the Blackburn Valley—one originally Great Central and the other, inevitably, Midland, for where one of these companies went in South Yorkshire the other, like Mary's little lamb, was also sure to go. A further approach to Barnsley was the ex-Midland link from Cudworth, notable for the Oaks viaduct which in its length of just over 1000 ft managed to cross two railways, two canals, a river and a main road! Still with us is the ex-Lancashire & Yorkshire line from Horbury through the twin single-bore tunnels at Wooley, but almost completely wiped off the map is the brave Hull & Barnsley Railway which never realised its ambition of breaking the North Eastern monopoly at Hull but did survive as an important coal artery until the late 1950s. Just south of Barnsley the now electrified line from Wath to Penistone through Wombwell with its 2-mile, 1 in 40 Wentworth bank was once the setting for some of the most spectacular steam operations in Britain. Westbound coal trains weighing over 800 tons would toil up the bank, often double-headed at the front and assisted at the rear by a conventional engine and the purpose-built 2-8-8-2 Beyer-Garratt No 69999, claimed to be the most powerful steam locomotive in Europe.

Further north are various ex-Lancashire & Yorkshire lines such as the 1 in 44 entry into Halifax from Greetland over which many steam-hauled freights required banking assistance; the direct link from Thornhill to Bradford through the characteristic millscape of the Spen Valley; and the important coal artery from Wakefield to Goole via Pontefract and Knottingley. But perhaps the most fascinating of all the secondary lines in the West Riding were those forming the once dense network of Great Northern suburban routes in the textile district. Here, before dieselisation or closure, would be seen N1 0-6-2Ts boldly blasting their way up the 1 in 40 to Howden Clough with three or four antiquated coaches *en route* from Wakefield to Bradford via Dewsbury; a J50 0-6-0T tackling the nightmare climb through Soothill tunnel outside Batley with a pick-up goods; or a J39 0-6-0 gingerly descending from Thackley with a Laisterdyke-Shipley (GN) freight, seemingly conscious of the fact that several locomotives have plunged through the buffer stops and on to the main road at the bottom. Pride of place must, however, be given to the lines from Bradford, Halifax and Keighley which converged at Queensbury, a unique triangular station 400 ft lower in altitude than the town it was supposed to serve.

West Riding branch lines in the strict sense of the term were in fact few and far between, but on one branch steam is still very much alive. This is the line from Keighley to Oxenhope, closed in 1962 but rescued by the Keighley & Worth Valley Railway Preservation Society and re-opened six years later just as steam on British Railways was fading into oblivion. Today it not only boasts a magnificent array of locomotives but passes through a landscape still faithfully reflecting the traditional atmosphere of the region. There could be no better setting to keep alive the glorious sight and sound of steam in the West Riding.

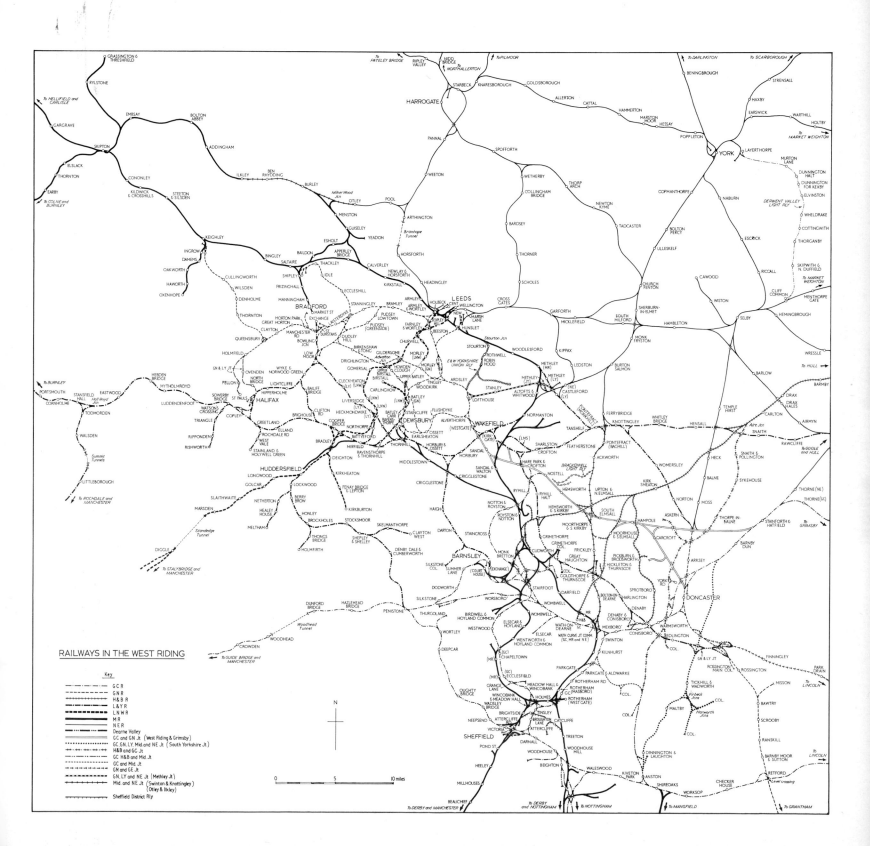

## RAILWAYS IN THE WEST RIDING

**Key**

| | |
|---|---|
| —·—·— | G C R |
| — — — | G N R |
| ········· | H & B R |
| ━━━━━━ | L & Y R |
| ▬▬▬▬▬ | L N W R |
| ━━━━━━ | M R |
| ▭▭▭▭▭ | N E R |
| —··—··— | Dearne Valley |
| —···—··· | GC and GN Jt (West Riding & Grimsby) |
| ···········| GC.GN.LY.Mid.and NE Jt (South Yorkshire Jt) |
| —·—·—· | H&B and GC Jt |
| —×—×—× | GC H&B and Mid Jt |
| —··—·· | GC and Mid. Jt |
| ——— | GN and GE Jt |
| ×××××× | GN, LY and NE Jt (Methley Jt) |
| ++++++ | Mid. and NE Jt (Swinton & Knottingley) (Otley & Ilkley) |
| ——— | Sheffield District Rly |

Scale: 0 ——— 5 ——— 10 miles

**THE MIDLAND TO CARLISLE**
Skipton, gateway to the Dales: a 9F 2-10-0
eases a northbound coal train away from the
station after taking water. The western edge of
Ilkley Moor can be seen to the right of the
picture.                                    *J. S. Whiteley*

A dirty and badly leaking Holbeck Stanier class
5 4-6-0 No 45080 heads south from Hellifield away
from the low afternoon sun on 18 March 1967
*G. W. Morrison*

Stanier class 5 No 44831 heads north through
Newlay Cutting on a Stourton-Carlisle freight on
10 June 1967.                                    *G. W. Morrison*

'Crab' 2-6-0 No 42900, one of those curious looking hybrids with Derby and Horwich parentage, accelerates through the outskirts of Sheffield with an evening stopping train from Sheffield Midland to Chinley.          *D. Penney*

*Above* Un-rebuilt Patriot No 45518 *Bradshaw* passes Shipley Leeds Junction with a down Leeds City-Morecambe express on 8 May 1962. The last half dozen members of this class finished their working life at Lancaster depot, mainly on Leeds-Morecambe trains. *G. W. Morrison*

*Top right* Class 4F No 44579 trundles past Calverley & Rodley with a mixed Skipton-Stourton freight on 27 February 1960. The locomotive is one of a few fitted with tender cabs. *G. W. Morrison*

*Bottom right* Class 2P 4-4-0 No 40538 prepares to leave Sheffield Midland with a local train to Chesterfield in August 1954. *P. J. Hughes*

The Fowler class 4F goods engines were nothing
if not versatile and were occasionally called on for
passenger duty.
Carrying express passenger headcode, class
4F No 44082 makes a spirited start from Leeds
City with a 10-coach excursion for Morecambe on
20 August 1960.                    *G. W. Morrison*

On the frosty morning of 4 November 1967
Stanier 8F 2-8-0 No 48074 disturbs the peace
of Ribblehead as it approaches the summit of the
Midland main line from Leeds to Carlisle at
Blea Moor.                                    *G. W. Morrison*

*Above*  On a bitterly cold November morning
a Stanier class 8F 2-8-0 emerges from Blea Moor
Tunnel on a northbound mixed freight. With the
meanderings of the county boundary after the
1974 local government re-organisation parts of the
West Riding in this area now fall within Cumbria.
*J. S. Whiteley*

*Left*  In June 1968 one of the last active 9F 2-10-0s
leaves the Midland route to Carlisle at Settle
Junction and takes the line to Carnforth with a
coal train.                      *J. S. Whiteley*

*Right*  The northbound Waverley crosses
Ribblehead viaduct headed by Jubilee class
No 45597 *Barbados.* 3 October 1959.

*G. W. Morrison*

Holbeck A3 No 60082 *Neil Gow* leaves Leeds City on the down Thames-Clyde Express on 3 March 1961. Nine A3s were transferred to Holbeck in 1960 to work the Midland Scottish expresses after being made redundant at Gateshead and Heaton by diesels. *G. W. Morrison*

*Left* The down Thames-Clyde Express climbing to Blea Moor between Horton-in-Ribblesdale and Ribblehead behind Holbeck rebuilt Scot No 46145 *The Duke of Wellington's Regt. (West Riding).* 3 October 1959. *G. W. Morrison*

**BRADFORD**
Low Moor Stanier class 5 4-6-0 No 44693 waits to
depart from Bradford Exchange with the up
Yorkshire Pullman. *G. W. Morrison*

*Above* Patricroft Caprotti BR standard class 5 4-6-0 No 73141, borrowed by Low Moor MPD to work the Bradford Exchange-Bridlington saturdays only express, storms up the 1 in 50 past St Dunstans on 1 July 1967. This was the longest regular out-and-back working for a crew on a steam locomotive by this date.    *G. W. Morrison*

*Right* Fairburn 2-6-4T No 42251 emerges from Hammerton Street Tunnel with a Kings Cross train. Tank engines were regularly used on these trains as far as Leeds or Wakefield where they were combined with the Leeds portion.

*G. W. Morrison*

*Left* Bradford Forster Square-Heysham parcels leaves behind Jubilee No 45697 *Achilles*. The unlined green Jubilee was running with a black lined tender from a Stanier class 5. 29 April 1967.

*G. W. Morrison*

*Above* The 15.40 stopping train from Bradford to Carlisle produced a variety of motive power, normally Kingmoor engines working back to Carlisle. Here, Britannia class 4-6-2 No 70051, formerly *Firth of Forth,* leaves Forster Square Station with the 15.40 in April 1966, shortly before the train ceased to run.  *J. S. Whiteley*

*Right* The up Bradford portion of the Yorkshire Pullman passes Laisterdyke behind Fairburn 2-6-4T No 42283. The Pullman Cars are the BR type built by Metro-Cammell in the late 1950s.  *G. W. Morrison*

*Above*  Carefully organised by the crews for the benefit of many photographers, the two 8.20 departures from Bradford Exchange to Bridlington and Skegness approach St Dunstans neck and neck on the 1 in 50 gradient behind Low Moor class 5s 44694 and 44662 on 26 August 1967. The Bridlington train on the left is being banked by a 2-6-4T.
*G. W. Morrison*

*Right*  On the damp and misty morning of 30 September 1967 the final steam-hauled Yorkshire Pullman climbs the 1 in 50 from Bradford Exchange to Laisterdyke behind the last B1 in active service, No 61306 shedded at Low Moor MPD. This was the final day of operation for the few remaining steam sheds in the West Riding. The leading two vehicles are in the blue/grey, grey/blue livery, only just coming into widespread use in the last year or so of steam working.
*G. W. Morrison*

*Left*  The climb out of Exchange as seen from inside the platelayer's hut near St. Dunstans. A B1 is heading a Kings Cross train.  *R. M. Lush*

## THE GN FROM KINGS CROSS

*Above*  The initial climb from Leeds Central to Copley Hill often proved difficult, particularly with a cold engine. Here class A4 Pacific No 60029 *Woodcock* slips furiously while heading the 17.00 to Kings Cross on 1 April 1962. The entrance to Wellington Street Goods Depot is on the left.

*J. S. Whiteley*

*Left*  With a guard and shunter as onlookers, Gresley A3 4-6-2 No 60062 *Minoru* starts a relief Kings Cross express from Leeds Central during the Christmas holiday of 1962.

*J. M. Rayner*

The Bradford portion of a Kings Cross-Leeds express sets off from Wakefield Westgate behind B1 No 61296 on 24 August 1961. *G. W. Morrison*

Preserved A3 Pacific No 4472 *Flying Scotsman* leaves its birthplace, Doncaster, with an excursion from Doncaster and Leeds to Carlisle and Newcastle on 1 June 1969. At this time it was the only steam locomotive permitted to run on BR.
*J. S. Whiteley*

*Right* Class A1 Pacific No 60145 *Saint Mungo* passes a deserted Copley Hill shed heading the 09.41 to Kings Cross in March 1963.
*J. S. Whiteley*

*Above left* Deputising for a failed Deltic, Peppercorn class A1 4-6-2 No 60145 *Saint Mungo* passes Beeston on the outskirts of Leeds with the up Queen of Scots Pullman on 7 June 1962.
G. W. Morrison

*Above* Fairburn 2-6-4T No 42073 passes Copley Hill depot with a freight from Wellington Street Goods Depot to Ardsley on 5 June 1963.
J. Hirst

*Left* Class J39 0-6-0 No 64796 ambles through Wakefield Westgate with a rake of empties for Ardsley on 24 August 1961.
G. W. Morrison

Thompson Class A2/3 Pacific No 60523 *Sun Castle* leaves Doncaster for Kings Cross on 29 April 1962. In the background can be seen the famous works, better known as the 'plant', while on the right an A1 waits as stand-by engine in case of failure on the main line.

*G. W. Morrison*

Class A1 Pacific No 60117 *Bois Roussel* starts the
17.10 to Doncaster away from Leeds Central on
25 April 1964.                    *J. S. Whiteley*

## SOME MOTIVE POWER DEPOTS

On view in the yard at Holbeck MPD, Leeds, on the murky morning of 17 March 1963 are Jubilees, 'Crabs', class 5s, an A3 and a standard class 5.

*J. S. Whiteley*

Fairburn 2-6-4Ts at Manningham.        *R. M. Lush*

Polmadie rebuilt Royal Scot No 46105 *Cameron Highlander* prepares to move off Holbeck depot to work the 10.35 to Glasgow St Enoch on 6 June 1962.

*G. W. Morrison*

Two standard class 4 4-6-0s and Holbeck 8F 2-8-0 No 48157 lined up outside Skipton on 20 August 1966.  *G. W. Morrison*

*Right*  Dwarfed by the power station, the inevitable WDs await their next turn at Wakefield.  *I. S. Krause*

Inside the roundhouse at Neville Hill, Leeds.
*I. S. Krause*

The stark mills, chimneys pointing skyward,
dominate this 1959 picture of Sowerby Bridge in
the Calder Valley with the motive power depot
in the foreground. On the skyline can be seen
Wainhouse Tower, a local landmark.

*G. W. Morrison*

## LEEDS

Edge Hill rebuilt Royal Scot 4-6-0 No 46124
*London Scottish* awaits the 'right away' from
Leeds City with a Liverpool express, having taken
over from an A3 which had brought the train
from Newcastle on 28 February 1960.

*G. W. Morrison*

Jubilee class 4-6-0 No 45695 *Minotaur* takes the
Manchester line at Leeds City Junction heading
the 8.45 Newcastle-Liverpool while a class
5 4-6-0 takes the Midland route and returns to
Holbeck MPD on 19 February 1963.

*J. S. Whiteley*

Fowler 4F 0-6-0 No 44044 passes Wortley
Junction with a northbound freight on 14 March
1962. The bridge in the background carried the
GN line from Wakefield and Bradford into Leeds
Central. _G. W. Morrison_

Immaculate Neville Hill A3 4-6-2 No 60086
*Gainsborough* stands ready to leave Leeds City
with the down North Briton for Edinburgh on
25 February 1961.                    *G. W. Morrison*

*Above* Austerity 2-8-0 No 90217 emerges from Marsh Lane cutting at Neville Hill West on an empty ballast train on 1 May 1962.

*G. W. Morrison*

*Right* Patricroft standard class 5 4-6-0 No 73039 storms up the newly installed link built as part of the Leeds rationalisation scheme from the Midland to the Great Northern and London & North Western lines on 8 July 1967 with a Saturdays only Newcastle-Llandudno train.

*G. W. Morrison*

*Below* Sunday afternoon at Leeds City shortly before reconstruction. Gresley class V2 2-6-2 No 60907 prepares to leave the east end of the station with the 14.45 to Newcastle in April 1962.

*J. S. Whiteley*

Not long before being withdrawn from service, unrebuilt Patriot No 45518 *Bradshaw* passes the site of Holbeck Low Level station with a Leeds City-Morecambe parcels train on 1 May 1962.
*G. W. Morrison*

Kingmoor Britannia No 70009 *Alfred the Great* pilots a standard class 4 4-6-0 out of Leeds with the Heaton-Red Bank empty van train on 11 April 1964. This regular working, usually heavily loaded, was the return of vans which had worked north to Newcastle overnight with newspapers from Manchester. *J. S. Whiteley*

*Right* Jubilee No 45562 *Alberta* passes Holbeck *en route* from Hunslet to Carlisle on its last working in normal service. A party from the Railway Correspondence and Travel Society are travelling in the front brake van. 30 September 1967. *G. W. Morrison*

*Above* Austerity 2-8-0 No 90503 passes Farnley Junction MPD on the LNW line to Manchester with an empty stock train on 28 May 1963.

*J. S. Whiteley*

*Left* Stockport Britannia No 70015 *Apollo* double-heads class 5 4-6-0 No 45200 out of Neville Hill yard on the Heaton to Red Bank empty vans on 3 July 1966. This train was normally loaded to more than 20 vehicles. *G. W. Morrison*

*Right* With the regulator wide open, class 9F No 92215 passes Holbeck MPD on a block train of oil tanker empties returning from Hunslet to Stanlow on 18 March 1967. *G. W. Morrison*

On a snowy 19 February 1963 Fairburn 2-6-4T
No 42188 approaches the GN line overbridge near
Whitehall Junction while heading a Bradford
portion of an express from St Pancras.

*J. S. Whiteley*

## THE CALDER VALLEY AND PENNINES

The Saturdays only Leeds-Llandudno passes Longwood & Milnsbridge as it battles up the seven miles of 1 in 105 from Huddersfield to Marsden on the LNWR route through the Pennines behind Jubilee No 45647 *Sturdee* on 20 August 1966.                    *G. W. Morrison*

*Right* Rebuilt Patriot No 45531 *Sir Frederick Harrison* emerges from Huddersfield Tunnel into the station on a morning Liverpool-Newcastle express. 27 September 1959.        *G. W. Morrison*

*Above* Alongside the Calder between Ravensthorpe and Mirfield an Austerity 2-8-0 No 90721 trundles along with a westbound coal train on 13 April 1964. *J. S. Whiteley*

*Right* Former Crosti-boilered 2-10-0 No 92021 leaves a smoke-screen as it struggles past Linthwaite on the climb to Standedge heading one of six special coal trains which ran on Whit Sunday 1966 from Healey Mills to the Manchester area. *F. J. Bullock*

An unusual motive power combination for this 20-coach empty stock train in the form of Austerity 2-8-0 No 90588 and Stanier 8F 2-8-0 No 48225 as it passes Golcar on 28 September 1963.
*G. W. Morrison*

Former LNWR G2 class 7F 0-8-0 No 49343 toils
up to Standedge tunnel with a Liverpool-Leeds
freight. It is seen here approaching Diggle, just
inside the West Riding boundary.      *K. Field*

Jubilee class 4-6-0 No 45600 *Bermuda* storms up
the bank out of Huddersfield past Paddock with a
Hull-Liverpool express on 4 July 1959.

*G. W. Morrison*

One of the last named B1s in active service,
No 61250 *A. Harold Bibby,* passes Mirfield MPD
with a westbound freight from Healey Mills on
26 February 1966.                    *F. J. Bullock*

*Right*  Class 8F No 48448 passes Heaton Lodge
Junction, Mirfield on a rake of coal empties from
Wyre Dock to Healey Mills. 6 April 1968.
                                    *J. S. Whiteley*

Crossing the West Riding boundary with Lancashire on a bitterly cold morning in December 1966, Jubilee No 45593 *Kolhapur* climbs the 1 in 80 to Copy Pit near Portsmouth on a special.

*G. W. Morrison*

Freights were often banked from Stansfield Hall
Junction, Todmorden, to Copy Pit summit on the
line to Burnley. Here two Stanier 8F 2-8-0s cross
the county boundary from the West Riding of
Yorkshire into Lancashire with a coal train, shortly
before the end of steam on BR.     *J. S. Whiteley*

**Top left** North of the Aire, BR standard class 4 No 75019 proceeds cautiously along the Grassington branch because of sheep on the line. It is heading for the limeworks at Swindon End where it will pick up a train of ballast. This was a working which survived to the end of steam in the area and attracted many enthusiasts.

*J. S. Whiteley*

**Left** The only member of the 842 Stanier class 5 4-6-0s to be fitted with Stephenson link motion although one of a few used for valve gear experiments, No 44767 accelerates a Leeds and Bradford-Liverpool express out of Halifax. 15 July 1959.

*G. W. Morrison*

## WEST RIDING MISCELLANY

**Above** On a crisp January day in 1963 class Q6 0-8-0 No 63445 passes through Bardsey on a Starbeck-Leeds freight.

*M. Mitchell*

*Above* Former Great Central class C14 4-4-2T No 67447 passes Nunnery Main Line Junction and heads down the Midland main line with a Sheffield Midland-Barnsley local. *K. R. Pirt*

*Top left* Former NER class B16 4-6-0 No 61429 and a Stanier class 5 4-6-0 take the Leeds line at Church Fenton with the Heaton-Red Bank empty van train in March 1959. *M. Mitchell*

*Left* Class D49 4-4-0 No 62738 *The Zetland* stands waiting to restart the Saturdays only 12.33 Harrogate-Leeds from Collingham Bridge in August 1959. *M. Mitchell*

*Right* In July 1968 a railtour organised by the Manchester Rail Travel Society is headed away from Hellifield by standard class 4 4-6-0s Nos 75019 and 75027 on the leg from Carnforth to Skipton. *J. S. Whiteley*

Britannia Pacific No 70013 *Oliver Cromwell* takes
the Penistone line out of Huddersfield at
Springwood Junction in October 1967 on one of
its many excursions in the latter days of steam.
*J. S. Whiteley*

Returning to home territory in East Anglia March
class B17 4-6-0 No 61627 *Aske Hall* makes heavy
weather of the 1 in 119 climb from Waleswood to
Kiveton Bridge soon after leaving Sheffield with
the Liverpool-Harwich boat train in September
1957
                                             *D. Penney*

*Above* On 25 September 1967 Jubilee No 45562 *Alberta* worked a special from Leeds to Beattock organised by the Jubilee Locomotive Preservation Society. Unfortunately the locomotive steamed badly all day and is seen here struggling towards Marsden on the climb out of Huddersfield.
*G. W. Morrison*

*Top right* Foreigner on the Settle & Carlisle: preserved WR Castle class 4-6-0 No 7029 *Clun Castle* struggles against the gradient and a strong westerly wind at the approach to Blea Moor on 30 September 1967 with a special excursion.
*J. S. Whiteley*

*Right* On 29 September 1963 Stanier Pacific No 46238 *City of Carlisle,* resplendent in red livery, made a fine sight at Dent backed by Widdale Fell while working a joint SLS/RCTS railtour.
*G. W. Morrison*

**WEST RIDING BRANCHES**

In BR steam days the service from Keighley to Oxenhope was worked by Manningham locomotives. Here Ivatt 2-6-2T No 41325 leaves Keighley in September 1959. Fortunately a member of this class has been preserved and can still be seen working on this line.

*G. W. Morrison*

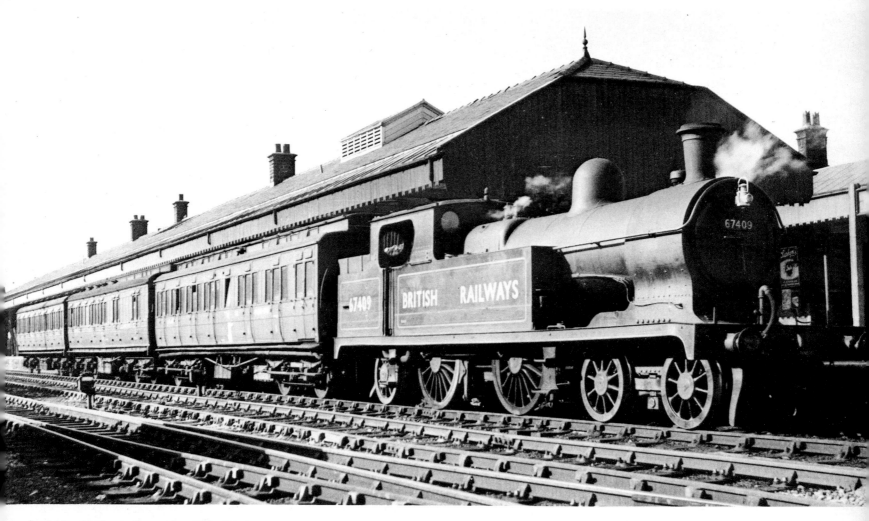

Penistone Station in September 1950. GC class
C13 4-4-2T No 67409 simmers quietly on a
Barnsley train. All three coaches are interesting
antiquities; the leading one is a Great Eastern
semi-corridor composite with clerestory roof, and
the second a GCR clerestory brake third.

*P. J. Hughes*

Steam in the West Riding in 1974. Preserved
Midland 4F No 3924 emerges from Mytholmes
Tunnel on the Keighley & Worth Valley Railway.
*J. S. Whiteley*

## ACKNOWLEDGEMENT

The authors would like to thank their fellow
photographers who have so kindly allowed them
to look through splendid selections of their work,
and whose kind assistance has, we hope,
produced a more balanced selection of pictures.